Memories of Ted Hughes

1952-1963

Memories of
Ted Hughes
1952-1963

Daniel Huws

· RICHARD HOLLIS ·

First published in 2010
by Richard Hollis
an imprint of Five Leaves Publications
PO Box 8786
Nottingham NG1 9AW
info@fiveleaves.co.uk
www.fiveleaves.co.uk

Second Impression June 2010

ISBN 978 1 905512 75 1

Designed and typeset by Richard Hollis

Printed by Short Run Press, Exeter

Five Leaves acknowledges financial support
from Arts Council England

A CIP record for this book
is available from the
British Library

I

In the autumn term of 1952, my first term at Cambridge, Dylan Thomas came to give a reading. The reading was in the Union. He read work of his own, but my clearest memory – remembered probably because the choice was to me unexpected – is of his reading of Auden's poem 'At Dirty Dick's and Sloppy Joe's'. Since that evening the poem, which I half knew, has remained in my head. That was the only time I remember seeing Dylan Thomas. Later, after I had come to know Ted, I would boast that Dylan used sometimes, as my mother told me, to come home with my father from the pub and sleep at my parents' flat in Anhalt Road, Battersea, about 1936-7, and I knew that after the war he was an occasional visitor to my father's flat in 18 Rugby Street, the flat Ted later lived in.

After the reading that night at Cambridge I called at the room of a friend in Pembroke College (my college was Peterhouse, over the road). Francis Holmes à Court had been at the same school as me, Bryanston. He, like me, but for different reasons, had been a misfit; he, shy, tall, big-boned and ungainly, I, also very shy, a boy who had come at fourteen from a Welsh county school in Llangefni. I quickly passed muster by being bright at science and maths and good at rugby; Francis loved his English literature and in his last year or two astonished everyone by taking to athletics and becoming the school's 440-yards champion. Francis was the only child of Lord Heytesbury, a kind and gentle man who lived in a modest house in Sevenoaks, which I once visited, and taught art at a local school. When I was about sixteen I began to read a lot of poetry, running quickly from Keats and Shelley to Eliot and Auden and Dylan Thomas. Francis was the only boy at school with whom I ever talked about literature. He had gone up to Cambridge a year ahead of me.

At Pembroke College on that autumn night in 1952, the two of us were sitting in Francis's room. Late, with great commotion, three or four students burst in and joined us. One of them was Ted, another was Terence McCaughey; I cannot be sure, though I could guess the names of the others. These had also been at the Dylan Thomas reading. Ted was animated. After the reading,

Dylan had been taken by the officials of the English Society (whose guest he was) to the Eagle in Benet Street, at the time a smart place to drink. Ted and his friends had followed, in the hope of being able to eavesdrop on Dylan's conversation, and had succeeded. Ted was full of the fantastical nature of what they had overheard. All I now recall is the fantasy of filling Swansea Bay with beer. I sat in the corner of the room and listened. When I got to know Ted, some time later, Dylan Thomas was still high in the pantheon, lower only than Shakespeare, Beethoven and Yeats.

Peterhouse was then, besides being the oldest, the smallest of the Cambridge colleges, and was reputed to have the best kitchen. Its student body was rather staid, or so I recollect. Several of its Fellows were known to be very famous, eminent historians and scientists, but none of them impinged much on student life apart from the gregarious Denis Mack Smith, a young Fellow. In a strategically placed room in the centre of the college, beneath Denis Mack Smith, was one of the most attractive and colourful of the Peterhouse undergraduates, Maurice Healy. Maurice was reputed to have got his Firsts in Classics without needing to work. He had been so well grounded by the good monks of Downside that he had won a scholarship to Peterhouse at sixteen, too young to go up, and had spent his last year at school being given enough additional teaching to carry him through his whole Tripos. Maurice was charming, laid-back, and knew everyone. He was a year ahead of me. I felt flattered when one night after Hall he suggested we go down to the Anchor for a drink. The Anchor, beside Queens' Bridge, was not a Peterhouse pub. It was at the time a run-down establishment. The interior of the small bar was painted in dark, glossy, smokestain-concealing brown paint. In a corner of the bar was a much-used hand-football machine. There were stairs leading down to a landing-stage in front of a boathouse where in summer there were tables and benches where one could drink, beside the punts in the water waiting for hire. There, that night, I was introduced to a circle of Pembroke students. Maurice knew them all but was not, I discovered, a habitué of that group. I however from that evening became a hanger-on.

The Anchor became my haunt. The custom was to gather in the Anchor before Hall and if nothing better offered itself to reassemble afterwards, this perhaps about twice a week. There might be occasional sorties to other pubs. The three of the company who stood out were Ted, Terence McCaughey and Roger Owen. Terence was Ted's closest friend, a Pembroke contemporary who also read English for part I of his Tripos, an Irish Presbyterian from Belfast, but a republican, a great story teller and mimic and singer. He it was who long afterwards gave the address at Ted's funeral. Roger was Liverpool Welsh, in his fourth year (doing a teachers' training course), an ebullient talker and theoriser. Roger had been one of the founders of the Cambridge weekly cyclostyled review, *Broadsheet*. He later worked for the BBC and later still settled in Israel with his second wife. Others were Brian Roberts, like Roger in his fourth year, later a school-teacher, and Cass (David) Morton, a scientist. They had mostly started as students of English and were now in their third if not fourth year. Ted, disenchanted with the university English course, had switched to anthropology for his part II. In those days he was by no means the main talker. That would have been Roger Owen; and next after him, probably, Terence. Ted would sit broodily, in the background, listening. But when he did come to speak, there would be an air of expectation, as if of an oracle. Whatever Ted came out with would be original, in a different key, gnomic perhaps, authoritative. Some topics, such as politics and sociology (beloved of Roger) did not interest him. English literature, naturally, figured often in the conversation; so did the teaching staff of the English department. The tone was one of irreverence. Leavis was often talked of, but simply because he provided good theatre, something of a buffoon. One went to his very crowded lectures (I went along a couple of times for the sport) in the hope of hearing some of his calculated, caustic put-downs, of T.S.Eliot or of George Moore or whoever. Anecdotes from Leavis lectures became part of Anchor lore. One of the few dons held in high regard was Matthew Hodgart, at Pembroke, whose interests embraced ballads and Joyce, a man who was at ease in the company of students. David Daiches used to be spoken of with some admiration (he was not one I even knew by sight) and, Terence tells me, Ted had thought highly of the lectures on Shakespeare by Hugh Sykes Davies.

Evenings began in talk and often ended in singing. Terence with a large repertoire of Irish songs and ballads was the chief singer. Ted, after a good deal of persuasion, would usually sing. He had a soft, light voice, with the slight tremolo which later characterized his reading voice. His *tours de force* were the ballads Sir Patrick Spens and Eppie Morie (learnt, I later realized, from Ewan MacColl records). He also had a couple of Yorkshire songs which he seldom sang and I do not remember, and now and again, Waltzing Matilda. On big nights, at weekends, we were sometimes joined by Macdonald Emslie, older than the others, a Pembroke research student in English who had been in the war and was already married. He was musical and would provide piano accompaniment. He later became the consultant musical editor of Pepys's diaries.

Two other hangers-on to the Pembroke group that year were Joe Lyde and Fintan O'Connell, both from Northern Ireland, both from Queens' College and, like me, then in their second year, the one a Protestant, the other a Catholic. Joe was cocky, sometimes very funny, often aggressively rude. He had in his first year been taken up as a sort of joker by the senior theatrical crowd. He played trumpet and jazz piano, and later had his own band, the best jazz band in Cambridge. His clarinetist was Dick Heckstall-Smith, who became a well-known professional. After Cambridge, Joe got a scholarship to Tulane University, for the sake of being able to play with bands in New Orleans (which he did). He returned to London and died young, of drink, the first of our contemporaries to die. Ted found him amusing in his uninhibited recounting of his escapades, and in his abrasiveness. Many, including Sylvia Plath, could not abide him.

What strikes me now, thinking about that group of Pembroke students which met at the Anchor, and making a comparison which might hardly have been recognised at the time, was how very provincial, in Cambridge terms, geographically and socially, it was. No doubt there were then at Cambridge (and perhaps still are) many comparable groups. Metropolitan undergraduate life hovered somewhere a few hundred yards distant from the Anchor, somewhere around Trinity College and Kings, around the theatre and the Union; its literary forum was the magazine *Granta*. One knew the stars by name and by sight: Peter Hall, Thom Gunn, Karl Miller, Peter Woodhouse, then Nicholas Tomalin, Claire Delavenay (later Tomalin), Sasha Moorsom, Judi Dench, Ronald Bryden. Ted had probably met a few of these, but neither he nor any of the Anchor people were so far as I was aware intimate with this world. The metropolitan centre was a place apart, a place to visit, a place to go in the evenings for entertainment – to a play, to see a film, one to come home from to talk about. The unpretentious provincial values of the

Anchor prevailed. Common to the company and no doubt a bond of sorts, if unrecognised, was the absence of public school presumptions, and so too probably its tenuous Celtic roots.

Girls seldom impinged on the life of most Cambridge male students. They were exotics. Female undergraduates were outnumbered by about ten to one. On rare occasions, Ted's girl-friend, Liz, a nurse from Manchester, would turn up at a weekend, a tall, blonde, pleasant girl. She smiled indulgently at the proceedings while she sat with us in a pub, and spoke little. Later, she emigrated to Australia and brought up a family there.

Ted had a large room under the roof on the eastern side of the first court at Pembroke. He had painted life-size pumas and other animals on the sloping surfaces. The story went that these had been reported to authority and that Mr Camps, the senior tutor, had come to see them for himself and to reprimand Ted, that Ted persuaded Mr Camps to lie down on the floor in order to appreciate them better. On his departure, Ted had to pay for them to be painted over. Ted had an excellent hand and eye and had observed acutely. He could from memory draw animals and birds with extraordinary detailed correctness; so too he could mould them from plasticine, as he used to do for our eldest daughter. Once Ted took me to the field over the river from Clare College to watch him practise his archery (he won a half-blue).

In his room Ted had a hired piano. He had taught himself to play, in order to play Beethoven sonatas. The best-known student poets of the day, as far as I can recall, were Thom Gunn and Fred Grubb. Ted is said to have met Fred Grubb one day and to have got into conversation and discovered a shared admiration for Beethoven. 'You must come up to my room and hear some', Ted told him.

Not long after I had come to know him, Terence took me to the University Library, a place which offered an ambience similar to the one in which I was to spend most of my working life, but a place that as an undergraduate I might otherwise have been slow to find my way to. David's marvellous second-hand bookstall in the corner of the market square with its ever-changing stock was enough in itself to furnish an education. The reason for Terence's taking me to the University Library was to read the only copy of *At Swim-Two-Birds* known to be in Cambridge (it had yet to be reprinted). The University Library had become the day-time haunt of Ted and Terence in their second year. It was a library which, unusually among the British copyright libraries, allowed readers access to the stacks. Ted could exhaust its shelves of folklore; he introduced me to some of his finds, among the favourites a collection of Bushman legends whose literal translations emerged, in their restricted English vocabulary, with a sort of Beckettian force.*

For a student such as Ted, already beyond anything the university curriculum could offer him, pursuing his own interests so hungrily, this enlightened policy of the Library must have been Cambridge's greatest contribution to his education. It was in those stacks that I discovered what wealth of traditional music was to be found in print. Ted used to say that whenever he entered the Library he

* The book was W. H. I. Bleek and L. C. Lloyd, *Specimens of Bushmen Folklore* (1911)

got an erection. The two splayed wings of the building, the vaginal entrance and the phallic tower had some complementary suggestiveness. What a tribute to the power of books.

Sometime in the Spring of 1954 I sent a poem, or perhaps poems, to the editor of a Cambridge literary magazine, *Chequer*. I received a note from him inviting me to tea in his room in Trinity Great Court. The editor was Ronald Hayman, later to become a biographer and the author of an opportunistic book about Sylvia Plath. This was my first and last meeting with him. I remember a stack of black curly hair, a pale face and a limp handshake. He accepted one poem. Some time in the summer term an issue of *Chequer* appeared in a bright yellow cover. In it was my poem, the first I had published. Soon afterwards, I met Ted one evening in the Anchor. He had with him a copy of *Chequer*. He had not known I wrote poetry. He pointed out another poem in the same magazine, by Peter Crew, and asked what I thought of it. My reply was I think on the whole favourable. 'I wrote it', he said. It had never crossed my mind that Ted might write poetry. He had, though I did not then know it (nor did any of his friends, not even Terence), by then published two other poems, in *Granta*, under the pseudonym Daniel Hearing. And as part of his Tripos exam, Terence told me, long afterwards, Ted wrote a masque (does it survive?). Also in that same issue of *Chequer* was a poem by Peter Redgrove. We knew Peter, but not well. He was a loner, a man marked by the then, in Cambridge, very uncommon fashion of short, cropped hair, given to wearing a black leather jacket, and was at Queens. Later that night Ted said 'Let's go and see Peter'. He was at home and was put to the same test as I had been. He had in his room a box of six bottles of German wine. We got drunk. Very late, we went out into the courtyard. There were signs of a party going on in a room high up in the old court. We crashed it and were given no welcome. Ted got in a tussle and hurt his thumb. For years after, that thumb gave him trouble.

The dress of Cambridge male students in the early 1950s would have struck later generations as remarkably conventional. Grey flannel trousers, tweed jackets and ties were the norm. A distinctive class, looked at with some disdain by many of the others, wore cavalry twill trousers and loud hacking jackets. Corduroys were still decidedly bohemian and blue jeans utterly exotic. A few, very few, for display or in eccentricity, dressed otherwise. Ted was never one to draw attention to himself. I find it hard to recall him dressed in anything other than grey flannel trousers and a black corduroy jacket. In cold weather he invariably wore a scuffed three-quarter-length leather coat which his uncle had worn as a soldier during the First World War.

The first poems of Ted to be published under his own name appeared, after he had gone down, in the following issue of *Chequer*, now edited by James Affleck and Neil Morris, in the autumn.

When I got to know Ted the poets he talked about frequently were Yeats, Blake, Dylan Thomas, Hopkins. In prose, Swift; the Swift of *A Tale of a Tub* and *A Modest Proposal* reigned supreme. Thoroughly absorbed, like

Shakespeare, but not much spoken of, were Wordsworth and Lawrence, *Sir Gawain and the Green Knight* and of course Child's ballads. Ted had been taught English by John Fisher, a friend of the poet Norman Nicholson who had edited a selection of Wordsworth's poetry. He used two copies of Wordsworth's collected poems to cut up for his selection. The two mutilated copies were given to Ted. If there was a favourite text at this time, it was Blake's *An Island in the Moon*. Ezra Pound and George Barker, two passing enthusiasms of mine, did not appeal to Ted at all. Nor, in those days, do I remember him ever speaking in admiration of Eliot, nor of Auden or of those then associated with him.

Later, in 1956, I developed a lasting love of Edward Thomas's poems. Ted shared this and wrote at least one very Edward Thomas-like poem at the time. When Ted returned from America at the end of 1959 we had, separately, both developed a passion for the poems of Emily Dickinson. In 1956 there were still gaps; by 1959 I suppose his knowledge of English literature was pretty complete and his exploration of modern foreign literature just beginning. It was Ted in 1960 who introduced me to the poetry of R.S. Thomas.

There was also the astrology. From the start, Ted talked about it. I must have been responsive. I learnt how to cast a horoscope and I read some books. I never came, as Ted did, in a way, to live by it, or at least to carry it in mind as some sort of parallel to actual life, aware from day to day of the changing planetary configurations. Ted, like a medieval poet, could see the black or the auspicious days coming and loved to let people know of them. But I took to the rich vocabulary astrology gave for discussing people. Freud and Jung were very much in the air at the time. Many of us read them. Their classification of people into types similarly extended the scope by which to talk about people, but in a more limited way.

II

Ted went down in the summer of 1954, and found work in London. He worked at various mundane jobs, one of them at London Zoo, the only job requiring literacy being one reading unsolicited film scripts at Pinewood Studios for Arthur Rank. He lived in 18 Rugby Street. My father, Richard Huws, had in 1946 – when he was released from war work and returned to London to freelance as an industrial designer – taken a flat on the second floor ('three knocks') of 18 Rugby Street. This was a small early Georgian house, one no doubt first intended as chambers, the odd one out at the end of a row of a slightly later and taller Georgian terrace. The inhabitants of the street at that time were still for the greater part locally born and bred, with a few slightly bohemian intruders. The rooms had original wooden panelling, much painted over. There was a pleasant small living room with two windows facing south onto the street, a bedroom at the back with space for a bed and in the front, off the living room, a room, if that is the word, about five foot square also with a fine view over the street, with a few shelves, a small working surface and a gas cooker: this space served as kitchen and bathroom. The only lavatory for the house was down under the pavement, the only water supply a tap above a tiny basin on a half-landing and the lighting was by gas lamp. One emptied a slop bucket. The whole block was part of the Rugby School estate. Rents were controlled, that of the flat about £2 a week, and the landlord understandably reluctant to make improvements. My father, now working elsewhere, passed the flat to me for my use and used it rarely as a pied-à-terre (he got on well with Ted). This flat was later Ted and Sylvia's first love-nest, and, again, their home for a few weeks when on their first return to London they stayed with us, and, mythologized, it is the subject of a poem in *Birthday Letters*. My wife Helga and I lived there from 1957 to 1961.

Two minutes walk from 18 Rugby Street, in Lamb's Conduit Street, was the Lamb. This had been my father's local and was that of all who stayed at number 18. Its public bar during most of the opening hours housed a regular clutch of winos drinking cheap draught cider. The saloon bar, in the evenings, drew an interesting mixture of people who lived in the area, some of them BBC, the most regular of them Bob Pocock. David Wright, the poet, who lived in Great Ormond Street, would be there most nights, often with his friend John Heath-Stubbs, now and again with their friend, George Barker. Ted and David Wright did not for some reason take to each other.

After going down from Cambridge Ted was strangely indecisive. He wanted to be a poet. Beyond that nothing was clear. He wrote a good deal, mostly poems, but sent nothing out for publication. So it remained until Sylvia came on the scene. Since he had come out as a poet, writing poetry had become a topic of conversation. Poems were occasionally exchanged. The aim in life was to write poems; the problem was how to find means of support. Ted would often now turn conversation to the question of how one could make money, other than by winning the football pools (which he used to try): by starting a herb farm, by keeping mink, or (he even took practical steps in this direction) emigrating to Australia to join his brother

Gerald. Ted dreamt that they might farm there. In his indecision, Ted seemed to cling to Cambridge and his remaining friends there. At weekends he would often be back.

The Anchor was still the habitual place of meeting. The Pembroke friends, with the exception of Terence, who stayed on for a fourth year doing Celtic studies, had now gone. The group which assembled there had transmogrified, had become more heterogenous. Three new faces were Colin White who was at Queens, reading English, and two from Christ's College, Roger Thompson, an architecture student, and John Hoare, also reading English. Colin was a lovable, fiery, passionate Scot and socialist (a nephew, he claimed, of Keir Hardie), but brought up in London. He and Roger and John had been together at Raynes Park School. Colin spent his summers working at Dounreay, where the atomic energy power station was being built, and in the bothies at Dounreay had picked up a repertoire of ballads and songs. Terence had the greater repertoire but several of Colin's, I later came to realize, were rarities, not to be found in print. I am proud still to be able to sing them. Colin went off soon after leaving Cambridge to teach English in Mexico. There he stayed, and married a Mexican Indian wife, and became a much loved university teacher.* Ted was fond of Colin and was one of the few friends (Daniel Weissbort was another) to meet him and his wife when many years later they made a visit to London.

*Obituary, *Guardian*, 11 March 2008

A new arrival at Pembroke who quickly became very attached to Terence was Hal (Harold) Bloom. He found the Anchor company congenial. Later, there came Lucas Myers, a singer of Tennessee songs, soon to become Ted's closest friend, and then three contemporaries from St Paul's School, David Ross, at Peterhouse, Daniel Weissbort at Queens and Than Minton at Trinity. Another face which became familiar end of that year was Michael Boddy, from Queens, trombonist in Joe Lyde's band, the bucolic 24-stone son of a vicar from the Yorkshire dales, the one utterly English member of our company, public-school in manner, amiable, suave, and one whose word could never quite be relied on. At the Anchor, Ted came to know all these. With Hal Bloom there was never rapport: they were too different, 'gods of dissimilar races'. With others, notably Daniel Weissbort, there developed in later years a close and lasting relationship. The ambience of Anchor evenings was now becoming more self-consciously literary.

Lucas Myers, drawn by the reputation of Dr Leavis, had chosen to come from Tennessee to Downing College. Maturer than most students – already a graduate of Sewanee and having worked as a merchant seaman – he quickly became disillusioned both with Leavis and with college life. He switched his subject, as Ted had done, from English to anthropology and moved out of college. He was allowed to make his home in a wooden hut, once a hen hut, in the garden of the rectory of St Botolph's in Newnham village. The unmarried rector lived in college, as a Fellow of Christ's. Helen Hitchcock, the eccentric widow of the former rector, still lived in the rectory, in one small room of her own, letting out the remainder of the house to some half dozen students. Here, in return for keeping the Aga boiler of the rectory stoked, Luke lived in his hut rent-free. He has written his own entertaining account of this interlude in his memoir printed as an appendix to Anne Stevenson's *Bitter Fame: a Biography of Sylvia Plath*.

Someone, I think at a party, had pointed Luke out to me. I introduced myself to him in the readers' canteen of the University Library and we quickly became friends. Luke, about the same time, was introduced to Ted by James Affleck and Neil Morris, editors of *Chequer*.

In the summer term of 1955 Ted quit London for the time being and pitched a tent in the garden of St Botolph's rectory. He found work on a rose farm. At the end of that term events unfolded – they are outlined in Luke's memoir – which met with the disapproval of college authorities. Luke was forbidden to return to his hut for the following term and eventually found digs in Tenison Road. This then became Ted's regular Cambridge pad. The hut at St Botolph's rectory was taken over by Helga Kobuszewski, who had arrived that May from Bonn University to spend a year in England and earn her keep by helping Mrs Hitchcock. I became the boiler-man and for my labour was allowed to have the small room that had been Helga's.

The Anchor remained the recognised place of rendez-vous. It must have been that summer that Ted met Shirley. She was an undergraduate at Newnham. She never joined the male company at the Anchor but would come and lean over the railings of the bridge. Ted would see her and be off. She was a tall, attractive, shy girl, with a farouche air. She is commemorated in Ted's poem 'Fallgrief's Girl-friends'. After being ousted by Sylvia she ever after, so far as I know, kept an honourable silence.

It was in David Ross's room at the end of that summer term of 1955 that the idea of publishing a poetry magazine was conjured up. The mock-serious title, *St Botolph's Review*, was proposed. David Ross was to edit it and he thought he could find the money to pay the printers (he was the only child of a generous father). The following year, 1955-6, saw the Anchor regulars much depleted.

Assembly there became less of a fixture. A new place of occasional meeting was Alexandra House, a newly opened coffee shop and eating house upstairs in an alley off Petty Cury. It was staffed by a bevy of young girls and the atmosphere was somewhat louche. The upper floor, where the girls lodged, became something of a doss house. One of the girls became David Ross's companion. Ted sometimes slept there.

St Botolph's Review was published on a Saturday, 25 February 1956. Contributors and friends sold copies on the streets and in cafes and pubs all day and in the evening came the party, a big party, held in the Women's Union, a large space on a first floor in Falcon Yard (again, off Petty Cury, a part of Cambridge that some years later was entirely demolished and turned into a shopping centre). I remember Sylvia coming in and crossing the room, with great verve, a most improbable partner to her companion, Hamish Stewart. Hamish, who walked with a habitual slouch, had a waxy, pale countenance and wore an affable, sheepish look accompanied by a slightly reptilian grin

('From what dog's dish or crocodile's rotten / larder she had come': Ted in 'Bawdry Embraced'), was a curiosity. We knew him as a frequenter of pubs; he was seldom sober and was thought to be an alcoholic. He was Canadian, said to be a son of the family that owned Johnson's Wax Polish.

Sylvia was new to us. Hamish made the introductions. Sylvia's first words to me were: 'And now I can meet your worse half', spoken with friendly aggression. They were fair retaliation for a facetious and wounding remark of mine writing in Broadsheet about poems of hers in a review of an issue of *Delta*, a serious-minded Cambridge literary magazine edited by Christopher Levenson (and previously by Philip Hobsbaum and before him Peter Redgrove). I was not witness to the drama of her meeting with Ted. Nor of Ted's punching a protesting Hamish.

After Easter 1956, those who still sometimes congregated at the Anchor, other than Luke, in whose lodgings Ted generally used to stay, saw less of him on his visits to Cambridge. Sylvia now occupied his mind. Ted kept her apart from his old friends. He must have been aware that to them, imbued with anti-American prejudice, she was the brash American girl who sought attention for herself in such unspeakable places as *Varsity* (the students' weekly newspaper), and that she of course would have felt singularly ill at ease among them. At the end of that summer term Sylvia's mother came over from America. She was on 16 June (as we were later to learn) to take part in the bizarre ceremony in the Church of St George the Martyr, Queen Square (the closest church to Rugby Street) in which Ted and Sylvia without the knowledge of family or friends, were to be married, as in a child's play wedding. That lay not far ahead. Meanwhile, under the impression that all Americans in those days were rich, the last verse of the ballad 'Mrs McGrath' which we had leant from Terence now ended 'For I'd rather my Ted as he used to be / Than with Sylvia Plath and her rich Mammy'.

Ted, now, with Luke, the oldest of us, began to assume more of a role of leader, to assert a moral authority, and develop his habit of laying down challenges. 'Write a poem about this', 'Do this'. He helped himself to three blank triplicate books (books for use with carbon paper) from his employer, kept one and gave one each to Luke and me, 'Fill this with poems'. Mine took ten or more years to fill. One challenge concocted between Ted and Luke that summer was to write a poem called 'Bawdry Embraced'. Luke wrote a good six-stanza poem which he never published, mine never got beyond one stanza, and Ted wrote the poem which, in Poetry Chicago, sent out by Sylvia, was his first professional piece of work. Though the poem was included in *Recklings* it is not in any Faber edition before the *Collected Poems* (where there is a note on its publication history). It was his existential celebration of the relationship with Sylvia, but written for his friends. Shirley was no doubt still a presence in the background. Ted, aware of what others might have been thinking about his abandonment of her, was putting on a show of bravado. A remark of his to Luke and me at the time portrayed this stance more crudely. To his prejudiced and disapproving friends he would not reveal the burgeoning literary symbiosis that was developing between him and

Sylvia. The truth of it, I would now guess, is that Sylvia was far more sexually experienced than Ted.

Sylvia records in her journal the remark about Ted by Hamish, a person who scarcely knew him: 'He is the biggest seducer in Cambridge'. Given Sylvia and Hamish's relationship at the time, the intended effect of his remark is obvious, though Sylvia may have taken it quite otherwise. But it did bring Hamish belated revenge. The words fell on fertile ground. They lent themselves to a view of Ted offered by a generation of writers about Sylvia. The only girlfriends of Ted's I was aware of before he met Sylvia were Liz and Shirley. To Sylvia I am sure he was loyal until Assia came on the scene. Later, finding himself in the wasteland of Crow, things changed.

III

Linda Wagner's draft of her book quoted from somewhere in Sylvia's writing her words, speaking of Ted, about passing through 'the mask of cruelty'. My comment was that Sylvia had hit on a truth. Ted was given to wild and fantastic and exaggerated talk and action – his friends regarded this as his chosen and proper style and expected it of him. A colouring of cruelty might at times be part of it. He could use it to shock people. And his manner was naturally blunt. But in this there was already a large element of acting a part, as though he wished to conceal his tender side. His stance in public, when not engaged, could be similarly misleading: still, with a watchful, guarded look. So could his regard for money: Ted had in him a Yorkshireman's respect for care, but his nature was extraordinarily generous. I was told that in the film made about Ted and Sylvia he is given to swearing. Never did I hear Ted swear; his use of language was always fastidious.

Ted, once he had come out as a poet, became more and more a promoter of other people's creativity, a forceful maker of suggestions, determined that people should turn their energy into creative channels. This trait throughout the remainder of his life many were to become aware of; a late example, shortly before he died, was his persuading Christopher Reid to give up his job at Faber: to save his soul, to get on with his own creative work. In the 1960s he persuaded David Ross to begin what may have been the first environmentally-conscious magazine, *Your Environment*; he sensed Daniel Weissbort's true bent and with him began the lastingly influential *Modern Poetry in Translation*.

At the beginning of the autumn of 1956, already married, but before Sylvia had broken the news of her marriage to her college and been allowed to live as a married woman, Ted lived in 18 Rugby Street, making frequent journeys to Cambridge. I was a registered research student and should have been living in Cambridge but had there a nominal address with an Irish landlord who forwarded mail; in fact I lived in London in 18 Rugby Street, making trips to Cambridge to see my supervisor. One day Ted said, 'You must translate Dafydd ap Gwilym'. He knew only Kenneth Jackson's translations in his *Celtic Miscellany*. On my next visit to Cambridge in Heffers bookshop, for 35/- (a big price in those days), I bought Thomas Parry's edition. I still have it, probably my most battered book. By the end of the autumn Ted had moved to Cambridge and soon afterwards I gave up research, and Cambridge, and went, with Helga, to join Luke and David Ross in Rome. We did not see Ted again until he returned to London with Sylvia in December 1959.

The Dafydd ap Gwilym translations, after my return to London, made slow progress and a few were published in American journals about 1959-60 (typed and sent out by Sylvia) but the projected book moved slowly and was eventually forestalled. I abandoned it the day I picked up in a bookshop Joseph Clancy's 1965 volume *Medieval Welsh Lyrics*. This contained a large selection of Dafydd's work, well translated, using, as I had done, the metre of the original. My knowledge of Welsh and of Welsh literature was at that time quite rudimentary; later, knowing far more, I should probably have been less bold. The familiarity with the text which my translations had given me simply became part of my education. Of manuscripts, which in later years were to become my métier, I then knew nothing. What neither I nor Ted could have foreseen was the new edition of the poetry of Dafydd ap Gwilym.* This succeeds that of Thomas Parry, and is, in so far as I contributed to its genesis and its text, indebted to that prompting of Ted's in 1956. But he no doubt would have set greater store by the translations than by a new edition.

* Edited by Dafydd Johnston, to be published in 2010.

The sub-tenant upstairs when Ted first lived in Rugby Street was Jim Downer, a young artist now working as an exhibition designer. Jim had drawn and written a children's book, *Timmy the Tug*. Ted offered to write a text for it in verse. The completed book, long lost and then found, was eventually published by Thames and Hudson in 2009, with a short memoir by Jim of his years in Rugby Street. Jim's friend, Peter O'Toole, then at the Bristol Old Vic, used to stay there on visits to London. He usually arrived with a girl or two in tow and hogged the floor.

By the autumn of 1956 Jim Downer and his girl-
friend, Wendy, had moved to a flat in Great Portland
Street. Ted and I were invited there for dinner. After dinner
Ted suggested that we should try the ouija board. Four of
us sat round. It was a new experience for me, a first and
last time. For what seemed ages nothing happened. The
spirit was summoned and no replies came, the glass
moved aimlessly around. The questioning was all by Ted.
Bored, in the end I started to provide answers. Ted
became quite excited. I became more and more nervous as
the questioning intensified. There came questions such as
where should Ted and Sylvia live? Where would they
write best? In America? I gave oracular answers. Who was
my favourite poet? Shakespeare. And my favourite line?
'Never, never, never, never, never'. Yes, and how does it go
on? I could not quite remember. Having time to think
(the whole process of pushing the glass about the board
allows plenty of that), I improvised: 'Why shall I ever be
perplexed thus? / I'd hack my arm off like a rotten branch
/ Had it betrayed me as my memory'. Ted was delighted.

Afterwards he talked about it. Only one thing wrong, Ted said (rightly, of course): Shakespeare would have written bough, not branch. I remember feeling utterly drained at the end of the session, as after a long game of chess played with determination to win. It made me wonder: was this what happened on other occasions with the ouija board? Ted persisting until one of the company, out of boredom or desperation or whatever, began to speak? And having started, had to find the inspiration to continue? The evening I describe appears as part of the poem 'Ouija' in *Birthday Letters*. The answers there described about football pools may have been from someone else on some other occasion. The 'poem' by the spirit which is quoted in *Birthday Letters* rings no bells in my memory though I fear it may have to be laid to my account.

During this same autumn of 1956 one last song was added to our repertoire, The Brown and the Yellow Ale, a rather marvellous one, which Ted loved, its English words taken from the Irish by James Stephens. We got the song from a BBC broadcast. It too comes into *Birthday Letters*.

Helga and I went to Italy after Christmas 1956, when I abandoned research. Ted and Sylvia went to America the following summer. We kept in touch by letter. Helga and I returned to London in August 1957, they in December 1959, accepting our invitation to stay at 18 Rugby Street. Jim Downer had been succeeded in the upstairs flat by Richard Hollis, a friend of Helga's and mine to this day. We had been offered a flat by friends and passed on the offer to Richard, who took it. And so it was that we became sub-tenants instead of him and possessors of a two-floor abode. Since 1956, 18 Rugby Street had come up in the world. There was now electric light and in the kitchens (those 5ft × 5ft spaces) running water and sinks, to which we added a hot-water gas geyser. Helga and I now slept in the airy upstairs flat. So Ted and Sylvia returned to the sagging net of the wide single bed which they had shared when they first came together.

Ted and Sylvia arrived in December, went up to Yorkshire for Christmas and after their return to London began their search for a flat. Sylvia was over six months into her pregnancy. My recollection of her in those weeks is stronger than that of Ted, partly perhaps because this was when I first got to know her quite well, and partly because of my memory of the intense energy and purposefulness she put into her hunting for a home. She would come back in the evenings exhausted. But she also relished the London bookshops. One evening she came home full of enthusiasm with a copy of Larkin's *The Less Deceived*. I remember this probably because of my surprise. Larkin was not one of Ted's enthusiasms and he seemed so un-American. Sylvia's interest had probably been roused by Robert Lowell, and Larkin's formal perfection, not something of great interest to Ted, of course appealed to her.

Given the edgy start to our relationship, I probably would have been placed by Sylvia in the same dubious category as most of Ted's friends had it not been for Helga. With Helga there was a quick rapport. There was the shared German background; Helga (in the difficult conditions of 18 Rugby Street) was domesticated and learning to adjust to life with a baby, as Sylvia also would soon have to do. There was the exchange of German recipes. Helga offered no literary rivalry. And they had in common the problem, as it sometimes became, of having to cope with their husbands' friends. Only now did I begin to become aware how great was Ted's own interest in food and cooking. Male student company had called for no interest or finesse. Ted, way back at the beginning of the 1960s, was the first person I remember talking of the perils of factory farming and of additives to foods. He had perhaps picked up some of this in America.

Whether Sylvia had altogether forgiven me my original offence I was never sure. Alone in her company, despite her warmth and enthusiasms, I could never feel quite relaxed (with Assia it was altogether different). Until the last time we met. It was in London, at a party, in November 1962 where I had not expected to see her. To my surprise, she lit a cigarette. I had never seen her smoke (any more than I had Ted). She said her lawyer had induced her to begin. She had been seeing him about the separation and the possibility of divorce and asked me what I thought, should they divorce? Shirking the difficult answer, I said that she would know what I as a Catholic believed, 'Till death do us part'. With great intensity Sylvia said, 'Yes, that's what I believe too'. She talked also of schizophrenia and her worries about her daughter, Frieda. In all ignorance (*The Bell Jar* was not yet published and Ted had kept silent) I said I thought it was usually hereditary. She said nothing. At the end, I left with Sylvia to find her a taxi. That was the only time we kissed and embraced (there was in Britain at that time much less social kissing and hugging than became common soon afterwards). My last sight of her was sitting bolt upright and staring ahead as the taxi vanished down the Kings Road. Soon afterwards she wrote a couple of very warm letters. Then I too, as everyone would do, inevitable though it may have been, managed to let her down.

After a couple of months in the Merwins' flat which had been lent to them, Ted and Sylvia's hunting was brought to an end with the taking of the small flat at 3 Chalcot Square, pleasant but cramped. Until we left for

Wales in 1961 we saw Ted and Sylvia, and soon Frieda too, quite often. We would generally meet in our homes, by arrangement, in small company, intimate and *gemütlich*. Sylvia could be at ease in such surroundings in a way she could not be, for instance, in a pub. We had glimpses of Sylvia's unreasonable possessiveness but never witnessed her rages, or were at the time even aware of them. Ted was always utterly protective, never complaining, never at that time telling anything about Sylvia's past. Ted and I, and others, would sometimes meet in pubs (mostly now in the Irish pubs of Camden Town). One rare occasion when Sylvia was with us in a pub, in Camden Town, was when Olwyn Hughes had come over from Paris on a visit. I still have a clear picture of Sylvia sitting erect and silent, wishing it were all over. The timeless, anarchic nature of pubs – a quality of Irishness, one might almost say (whether the pub was Irish or not) – something Ted loved, in his younger days, was anathema to Sylvia, with her strong need to feel that everything was under control, even her social pleasure, and with her businesslike dedication of her time.

On their way to Bangor in July 1962, together again for a while after their first split, Ted and Sylvia spent a night with us in Penrhyncoch. Helga and I heard something of the trouble between them. Ted and I went for a walk and I was told of his having discovered his 'dark muse'. Helga was also told about her, by Sylvia, but told at the same time, rather oddly, how Sylvia and Ted had never spent a night apart. Yet neither Helga nor I remember that evening as being a gloomy one.

After Sylvia's death Ted was convinced that were it not for the several bad strokes of fortune just before her suicide, she would be alive, and that they would have been reconciled. To think this was human. The re-colouring of the past that we are all given to had begun. It lies heavily over *Birthday Letters*. Ted also said at the time that had they been poorer, had he had to earn a living by a daily job and live a routine life, the marriage would have been saved. But both Ted and Sylvia knew that being poets, ambitious poets, the stakes were high. They knew their poetic myth: Ted with cool clear-sightedness, Sylvia, as her dream-house shattered, discovering its reality with sudden hallucinatory clarity. Ted's radio play 'Difficulties of a Bridegroom', broadcast in January 1963, contained a pre-figuration. The event behind it was real. Ted drove up to London from Court Green, ran over a hare on the way, sold it to the butcher in Lamb's Conduit Street and with the money he received bought roses. It must have been hard ever after for Ted to bring himself to think about that broadcast. It echoes in Sylvia's last poems, her 'Greek necessity'.

Afterword

For some time I felt that I owed it to Ted's memory to write down as a matter of record what I remembered of him in the early years of our friendship. For this reason, deliberately, I did not read Elaine Feinstein's biography. Over the years however I had read some of the early books about Sylvia and many subsequent articles in newspapers. I had seen how Ted's character had been traduced and how a highly distorted picture of him, which derives in part from Sylvia's letters and journal and in part from more dubious sources, came almost unquestioningly to be regarded as a true one. When an invitation came to write something about Ted, for a book to celebrate the tenth anniversary of his death (a book which aborted), I was grateful to be stirred into action.

When Linda Wagner-Martin began to write her biography of Sylvia (published as *Sylvia Plath: a Biography* in 1987), Ted's sister Olwyn urged several of his friends, who might not have chosen to do so, to co-operate with her. Olwyn soon changed her mind about Linda Wagner. In the meanwhile, however, I had written to her some comments on a draft of her book which she sent me (not much of what I wrote turned out to fit her thesis). Anne Stevenson in *Bitter Fame* made better use of a copy of the same comments. Some of the memoir published here is derived from what I then wrote, at a time when my memory may have been a little sharper than now.

Not long after I had written this essay *Letters of Ted Hughes* was published. Some of my recollections may appear unilluminating when read beside what Ted in his letters has to say about his early poetic development. I have nevertheless let my text stand. It has benefited from conversation about Ted with Terence McCaughey and from comment by Lucas Myers on a draft.

Daniel Huws was born in London in 1932, his mother English, his father Welsh. He spent much of his childhood in Wales. From 1961 to 1992 he worked in the Department of Manuscripts of the National Library of Wales. Two collections of his poetry have been published, *Noth* (London: Secker & Warburg, 1972) and *The Quarry* (London: Faber & Faber, 1999).

Daniel Huws has written extensively, in English and Welsh, on Welsh manuscripts and on Welsh traditional music. In 2006 he was awarded the Derek Allen Prize for Celtic Studies by the British Academy.

Also published
by Richard Hollis and Five Leaves

Susan Alliston
Poems and Journals
1960–1969
Introduction by Ted Hughes

. . . "a weird blend of something
savage and a bit surreal with a hard, fine
conscientious realism".
– Ted Hughes, 1970